NUMBERS 1–20

Know Your Numbers

FOOD

Mary Elizabeth Salzmann

Consulting Editor, Diane Craig, M.A./Reading Specialist

Sandcastle

An Imprint of Abdo Publishing
www.abdopublishing.com

visit us at www.abdopublishing.com

Published by Abdo Publishing, a division of ABDO, PO Box 398166, Minneapolis, Minnesota 55439. Copyright © 2015 by Abdo Consulting Group, Inc. International copyrights reserved in all countries. No part of this book may be reproduced in any form without written permission from the publisher. SandCastle™ is a trademark and logo of Abdo Publishing.

Printed in the United States of America, North Mankato, Minnesota
062014
092014

THIS BOOK CONTAINS
RECYCLED MATERIALS

Editor: Alex Kuskowski
Content Developer: Nancy Tuminelly
Cover and Interior Design: Anders Hanson, Mighty Media, Inc.
Photo Credits: Shutterstock

Library of Congress Cataloging-in-Publication Data
Salzmann, Mary Elizabeth, 1968- author.
  Know your numbers. Food / Mary Elizabeth Salzmann.
    pages cm. -- (Numbers 1-20)
  Audience: Ages 3-9.
  ISBN 978-1-62403-265-3
1. Counting--Juvenile literature. 2. Cardinal numbers--Juvenile literature. 3. Food--Juvenile literature. I. Title. II. Title: Food.
  QA113.S293 2015
  513.2--dc23
              2013041909

SandCastle™ Level: Beginning

SandCastle™ books are created by a team of professional educators, reading specialists, and content developers around five essential components—phonemic awareness, phonics, vocabulary, text comprehension, and fluency—to assist young readers as they develop reading skills and strategies and increase their general knowledge. All books are written, reviewed, and leveled for guided reading, early reading intervention, and Accelerated Reader® programs for use in shared, guided, and independent reading and writing activities to support a balanced approach to literacy instruction. The SandCastle™ series has four levels that correspond to early literacy development. The levels are provided to help teachers and parents select appropriate books for young readers.

EMERGING · **BEGINNING** · TRANSITIONAL · FLUENT

Contents

Watermelon	4		Spices	14
Oranges	5		Muffins	15
Corn on the Cob	6		Squash	16
Milk	7		Cherries	17
Cake	8		Bread	18
Hot Dogs	9		Green Beans	19
Apples	10		Peas	20
Cookies	11		Pepperoni	21
Tomatoes	12		Gummy Bears	22
Raspberries	13		Asparagus	23
			Glossary	24

Brandon is at a **picnic**. He eats
1 piece of watermelon.

Trisha cut an orange in half.
Now she has 2 halves!

•• = 2 = two

1 2 3 4 5 6 7 8 9 10 11 12 13 14 15 16 17 18 19 20

Josh eats a piece of corn. There are
3 more pieces on the **grill**.

••• = 3 = three

1 2 **3** 4 5 6 7 8 9 10 11 12 13 14 15 16 17 18 19 20

Four girls drink 4 glasses of milk.
Hannah has a milk **mustache**!

●●●● = 4 = four

1 2 **3** **4** 5 6 **7** 8 **9** 10 **11** 12 **13** 14 **15** 16 **17** 18 **19** 20

It is Chris's birthday! He serves
5 pieces of cake.

●●●●● = 5 = five

1 2 3 4 5 6 7 8 9 10 11 12 13 14 15 16 17 18 19 20

Emma and Alex love hot dogs.
Their dad **grills** 6 hot dogs.

●●●●● = 6 = six

1 2 3 4 5 6 7 8 9 10 11 12 13 14 15 16 17 18 19 20

There are 7 apples. Jimmy bites
a red apple.

●●●●● ● = 7 = seven

1 2 3 4 5 6 **7** 8 9 10 11 12 13 14 15 16 17 18 19 20

Jack and Ava help bake cookies.
They have 8 cookies.

●●●●●●●● = 8 = eight

1 2 3 4 5 6 7 8 9 10 11 12 13 14 15 16 17 18 19 20

The **tomatoes** are on a **vine**.
There are 9 tomatoes.

●●●●● = 9 = nine

1 2 3 4 5 6 7 8 9 10 11 12 13 14 15 16 17 18 19 20

Zoe has 10 raspberries. She puts
one on each finger.

●●●●● = 10 = ten

1 2 3 4 5 6 7 8 9 10 11 12 13 14 15 16 17 18 19 20

13

Spices make food tasty! Can you count the spices?

⣿⣿ = 11 = eleven

1 2 3 4 5 6 7 8 9 10 **11** 12 13 , 14 15 16 17 18 19 20

Grace and Ryan like to cook.
They made 12 **muffins**.

●●●●●
●●●●●
●● = 12 = twelve

1 2 3 4 5 6 7 8 9 10 11 **12** 13 14 15 16 17 18 19 20

Squash come in many different shapes. There are 13 squash.

⬤⬤⬤⬤⬤
⬤⬤⬤⬤⬤
⬤⬤⬤ = 13 = thirteen

1 2 3 4 5 6 7 8 9 10 11 12 **13** 14 15 16 17 18 19 20

The cherries come in pairs.
There are 14 cherries.

= 14 = fourteen

1 2 3 4 5 6 7 8 9 10 11 12 13 **14** 15 16 17 18 19 20

17

The bread is cut into **slices**. How many slices do you see?

1 2 3 4 5 6 7 8 9 10 11 12 13 14 **15** 16 17 18 19 20

This family is made of vegetables.
There are 16 pieces of green bean.

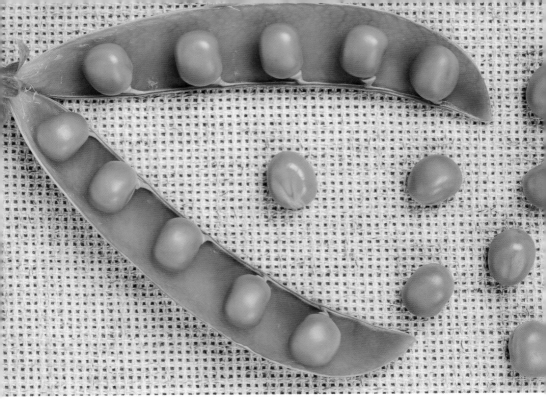

Peas grow in pods. This pod has 17 peas.

= 17 = seventeen

1 2 3 4 5 6 7 8 9 10 11 12 13 14 15 16 **17** 18 19 20

Mike and Ben share a pizza. It has
18 pieces of **pepperoni**.

= 18 = eighteen

1 2 3 4 5 6 7 8 9 10 11 12 13 14 15 16 17 **18** 19 20

Gummy bears are sweet! There are 19 gummy bears.

= 19 = nineteen

1 2 3 4 5 6 7 8 9 10 11 12 13 14 15 16 17 18 **19** 20

Kylie cooks **asparagus**. She has
20 **spears**.

 = 20 = twenty

1 2 3 4 5 6 7 8 9 10 11 12 13 14 15 16 17 18 19 **20**

Glossary

asparagus – a green plant that grows spear-shaped stalks that can be cooked and eaten.

grill – 1. a device with metal bars on which food is cooked. 2. to cook food on a grill.

muffin – a small cake or bread that is baked in a cup-shaped container.

mustache – the hair that grows on the upper lip.

pepperoni – a type of hard Italian sausage that is seasoned with pepper.

picnic – a meal eaten outdoors, often while sitting on the ground.

slice – a thin piece cut from something.

spear – a long shoot or stalk of a plant such as asparagus.

tomato – a soft, red fruit that is eaten as a vegetable. It can be eaten raw or cooked.

vine – a plant that has a long stem that grows along the ground or clings to things such as trees.